AF095646

IT'S TIME TO EAT BLACKBERRY PEEKABOO COOKIES

It's Time to Eat BLACKBERRY PEEKABOO COOKIES

Walter the Educator

Silent King Books
A WhichHead Entertainment Imprint

Copyright © 2025 by Walter the Educator

All rights reserved. No part of this book may be reproduced in any manner whatsoever without written per- mission except in the case of brief quotations embodied in critical articles and reviews.

First Printing, 2024

Disclaimer

This book is a literary work; the story is not about specific persons, locations, situations, and/or circumstances unless mentioned in a historical context. Any resemblance to real persons, locations, situations, and/or circumstances is coincidental. This book is for entertainment and informational purposes only. The author and publisher offer this information without warranties expressed or implied. No matter the grounds, neither the author nor the publisher will be accountable for any losses, injuries, or other damages caused by the reader's use of this book. The use of this book acknowledges an understanding and acceptance of this disclaimer.

It's Time to Eat BLACKBERRY PEEKABOO COOKIES is a collectible early learning book by Walter the Educator suitable for all ages belonging to Walter the Educator's Time to Eat Book Series. Collect more books at WaltertheEducator.com

USE THE EXTRA SPACE TO TAKE NOTES AND DOCUMENT YOUR MEMORIES

BLACKBERRY PEEKABOO COOKIES

It's time to eat, hooray, hooray!

It's Time to Eat
Blackberry Peekaboo Cookies

Blackberry cookies are on the way.

Peekaboo filling, purple and sweet,

A tasty cookie, ready to eat!

Round and soft, with a little hole,

The blackberry jam peeks out like gold.

Peekaboo cookies, what a sight,

A yummy treat that feels just right!

One for you and one for me,

How many cookies can we see?

Let's count them up, one, two, three!

All so tasty as can be.

Take a bite and peek inside,

The jam is there, it cannot hide!

Sweet and sticky, purple fun,

Peekaboo cookies for everyone!

It's Time to Eat
Blackberry Peekaboo Cookies

Circle cookies, soft and round,

With blackberry jam all safe and sound.

Peekaboo giggles, peekaboo cheer,

Blackberry cookies are finally here!

Dip in milk or eat them plain,

Each sweet bite is like a game.

Peekaboo jam says, "Hello you!"

What a cookie, soft and goo!

Pass the plate and grab some more,

Cookies, cookies, what a score!

Blackberry peeks from every one,

Peekaboo treats are so much fun.

Crunchy edge and fruity heart,

Blackberry cookies are true art.

With every bite, we laugh and chew,

It's Time to Eat
Blackberry Peekaboo Cookies

Yummy, yummy peekaboo!

When they're gone, we lick our lips,

No more crumbs or cookie bits.

But next time, we know what to do,

Bake some more sweet peekaboo!

Now we clean and wash our hands,

Snack time over, wasn't it grand?

Blackberry Peekaboo made us smile,

It's Time to Eat
Blackberry
Peekaboo
Cookies

We'll have them again in just a while!

ABOUT THE CREATOR

Walter the Educator is one of the pseudonyms for Walter Anderson. Formally educated in Chemistry, Business, and Education, he is an educator, an author, a diverse entrepreneur, and he is the son of a disabled war veteran. "Walter the Educator" shares his time between educating and creating. He holds interests and owns several creative projects that entertain, enlighten, enhance, and educate, hoping to inspire and motivate you. Follow, find new works, and stay up to date with Walter the Educator™

at WaltertheEducator.com

www.ingramcontent.com/pod-product-compliance
Lightning Source LLC
La Vergne TN
LVHW052010060526
838201LV00059B/3960